DEDICATION

To Olga Ozwinsky, who had the gumption to kick,
while those around her hand balled

Contents

FORWARD BY JVG

I can't remember how long Ian's been reading his
poems on my radio show. About half as long as I've
been doing the show I'd reckon. I've been doing the
show about 20 years. Do the math.

I have no idea how he comes up with what he comes
up with. Every week a new poem. Usually funny,
regularly insightful, often epic (read 'long') and more
often than not rhyming. It's a curious and rare talent.

Occasionally strangers ask me about my show and by
far and away the most asked question is, "How does
that poet bloke come up with a new poem each week?"

One day someone told me how he turns off the lights,
draws the curtains, lies on his bed and closes his eyes
to listen to Ian's segment every Sunday afternoon. No
doubt an expression of his passion for Ian's work.
Possibly a bit too much information though.

Doing the radio with Ian is a pleasure but what I
really enjoy is when we go and do gigs up the country
and Ian reads his poetry to people who've never heard
of him before. I watch these people, regular folk who
lap it up like they've never lapped up poetry before.
He'll start reading and he'll silence a coastal bowling
club. All ears on Ian and his genius doggerel. That's
when you know he's on to something.

Jon Von Goes.

FORWARD BY BRIAN NANKERVIS

A few summers ago a friend and I spent a wonderful day with Ian. It was like living inside one of his poems. Long and languorous, intelligent, funny, mysterious, uniquely Australian and refreshingly honest ... with an unexpected twist at the end when we insisted on driving him home rather than dropping him at the station as he'd requested. We wanted more! More stories, more wise counsel from the back seat, more shared wonder at the whims of this topsy turvy world.

Ian and I were performing as part of a fabulous show at the Barwon Heads Community Centre with Chris Wilson, Sarah Carroll and one of our favourite bands, The JVG Guitar Method. Hot weather was predicted so we left Melbourne early to have a swim at Ocean Grove, a leisurely post body-surf lunch and a wander around the cliffs at Point Lonsdale. The night was a ripper but the highlight was Ian's show stopping poem about a grudge football match between the Razor Hill Vultures and the Coffin Bay Boners, umpired with breathtaking creativity under pressure by Stan Gooch, a proud proctologist not afraid to closely examine Lester 'Bluetongue' Izzard. Hilarious. Outrageous. Very hard to follow!

Grand Final day at Sulphur Creek
The mood at best, was tense
The medics carried mace
Barbed wire secured the fence

In 2010 I watched, spellbound, as Ian captivated a full house at St Kilda's beautiful Palais Theatre with a poem that truly spoke to the heart of St Kilda. A poem celebrating the essence of that complicated suburb with humour and topicality ... and then cutting to the core of why we were there, raising money for those who were doing it tough ...

The homeless, the damaged, dispossessed, self inflicted
Those who've lost hope, the abused, the addicted
Are met, not in judgement, not in shame or despair
The true heart of St Kilda – is the people who care

I've loved Ian's BBQ Day songs and poems and marveled at the marvelous word play and the clever rhythms and rhymes ... you have to be happy with parodies like 'You Just Like Me 'Cos I'm Good In Bread', 'I've been contemplating silverside'

I listen to Ian's poems on the JVG Radio Method every Sunday afternoon on Melbourne's fine community radio station, Three Triple R and at the occasional live gig ... but at last I can dip in and out of Ian's collected works in a book! There are poems here to make you laugh, poems to cast new light on the familiar, poems to inform, challenge and inspire. Poems of real heart and soul, companions for the road, the home and beyond.

Thank you Ian!

Brian Nankervis.

FOREWARD BY IAN BLAND

At the beginning of 2007, Jon Von Goes invited me to present a weekly spoken word segment on his radio program "The JVG Radio Method" and the brief was, well, brief.

My offering must be "thematically correct", the segment would be titled "Bland on Bland" and the theme for the following week would be emailed, texted or delivered by courier pigeon a few days prior, technology dependant.

Most of the pieces presented here have been re-visited since they went to air, though not rebuilt; I have combed their hair and pulled up their socks but left them wearing the same dirty clothes.

Ed Bates, take a bow.
Each week Ed drags himself away from his suburban vegie patch to baste my verse and Dan Warner's songs with his superlative lap steel playing.

Until the first note emerges I'm never sure what's going to come out.
Frankly, I don't think he does either.

All the Radio Method regulars, Jon Von Goes, Dan Warner, Dr Pump, Keith Fuller, Pete Ewing, Sarah Carroll, Dave Evans, Nathan Farrelly, Jane Hendry, Jed Macartney, and the hundreds of guest performers who make it a joy to be part of 'The JVG Radio Method'.

Thatch and Jools for this book, the website and various other black arts, enabling me to contribute each week while on the road despite my Luddite inclinations.

Nic and Ellen, for their encouragement and for tolerating me stuffing up their weekends.

Community radio in general and RRR in particular; all those who listen, contribute and subscribe, encouraging young and old to experiment, develop and present ideas unthinkable on commercial networks.

Finally, those I've conversed with in pubs; those I haven't met or even seen, whose discussions I've overheard on trains, trams and busses; those who sell The Big Issue and share their stories; those I've passed in the street or stood behind in a queue who have unwittingly revealed more about themselves in a glance than any conversation would divulge.

Those whose personalities, mannerisms, prejudices and turn of phrase have drifted into these verses, giving sinew and breath to the characters, proving, if ever there was doubt, as much intellect, wisdom and wit reside in an Op Shop frock or pair of overalls as any Italian suit.

Ian Bland.

IAN BLAND

A LOVE SONNET FOR A DOG

I suppose our dog's alright;
perhaps a little too demanding
I wouldn't call it love; still,
we've reached an understanding

She rules the house and backyard;
I'm left the garden shed
She owns the couch till 10pm,
then she claims the bed

She's sharp as a dugong's armpit;
thicker than mountain fog
But I can't fool her which reveals more
about me than the dog

We've nothing much in common:
In life you take what comes
I like reading Proust;
she likes sniffing bums

She doesn't like my music,
makes that very plain
A patronising glance
blending pity with disdain

Yawns and rolls her eyes:
Reckons she's so smart
Scratches round her nethers
Then drops a massive fart

Ignores me until dinner,
When suddenly I'm the man

I quip, "You reckon you're so clever,
Here, you open up the can."

She whines to be let out,
She whines to be let in
She whines so much I've dubbed her
The "four legged violin"

It's like a marriage of convenience
To a fractious, moody spouse
Still it's nice to see her hairy face
Shuffling round the house

I believe, at heart, she's happy;
To be honest, she'll do me
If only I could teach her
To make a decent cup of tea

ALCOHOL

Henry loved his alcohol
Fired the heart and soothed the soul
So much so he claimed it was divine

No other liquid had such class
Each drop, religion in a glass
Didn't Jesus turn water into wine?

"Holy water," Henry's thinking
"Endless uses, not just drinking
To be cherished in all its many forms

A scan of labels, packs and jars
Brought a pant of oohs and ahhs
"It moisturises, bleaches, whitens, warms

Used in mouth wash and cosmetics
Repellents, diuretics
Stain remover, lip gloss and shampoo

Sunscreen and pain relief
Cleans your car and cleans your teeth
Is there anything that alcohol can't do"?

Grog was his Achilles Heal
Before and after every meal
From when he woke until when he went to bed

It so upset Valmae, his wife
Who warned his ways would end in strife,
"Keep this up, doctor says you're dead"

Henry fumed with indignation
"I only drink in moderation
So I like a nip, is that a sin"?

"You can't link my diabetes,
With pouring sherry on my Weeties,
Doesn't everybody dunk their toast in gin?"

Liqueurs, spirits, cocktails, ciders
Aperitifs, vodka spiders
For vitamins he'd add tomato juice

Pork ribs with whiskey glaze
Tequila in the mayonnaise
Val gave up, crying, "Henry, what's the use"?

In due time, vascular disease
Claimed both legs at the knees
But Henry's lifestyle didn't miss a beat

He tried to drink the anaesthetic
Refused to wear his new prosthetic
"To drink," he scoffed, "You don't need bloody feet"

The end was sudden, when it came
Twelve martinis to his name
They found him with the glass still to his lip

Though his blood was point three five
Despite the grog, he'd be alive
If he hadn't choked on an olive pip

He willed his body laid out nude
In a vat with hops and brewed
Or bathed in cloves and wine and slowly mulled

But his widow wasn't thrilled
Valmae preferred he be distilled,
"I'd rather he was sipped instead of skulled"

Henry got his wish at least
They stuffed his body full of yeast
Fermented him, then stored him in a cask

Though he was a little pale
Henry made a splendid ale
What more could any tippler ask?

Henry's final hours were spent
A little over ten percent
A full strength brew by anybodies measure

Instead of ashes or a vault
Henry's spirit fused with malt
If only more of us could give such pleasure

ALRIGHT

The task appeared quite simple;
At least it did to me
Sanitary pads, regular,
And a packet of mint tea

Alright, I should have been prepared;
Thanks for the advice
But my French-English Dictionary
Wasn't that precise

I'd mastered the important words;
I'd practiced for a year
Cognac, Cidre, Champagne,
Vin Rouge, Vin Blanc, une Biere

Beer, cider, champagne, cognac,
Wine; red and white
Thank you, hello, beer, cider,
Wine, yes, alright

I should have learnt the word for "no";
In hindsight I concede
But a hedonistic holiday?
Not a word I thought I'd need

Besides, there's a language
The whole world understands
The universal language:
Gesture with your hands

I addressed them in their native tongue,
Perhaps my vowels were slurred

The response was animated,
Though I didn't catch a word

All attempts to clarify were met
With howls of laughter
They offered countless products,
Though none I was after

I gestured with my fingers,
My buttocks, legs and arms
A little too explicitly
Or so said the gendarmes

Not wanting to seem ignorant
And sensing a rapport
I replied, "Alright, alright, alright,
D'accord, d'accord, d'accord"

At least I've brought home something,
Not exactly what you want
Fourteen tubes of haemorrhoid cream
And a bottle of crème de menthe

I've narrowed my French to a single sentence;
Concise, direct, polite,
"Je ne parle pas Francais, d'accord?
I don't speak French, alright?"

BALL

There's a scene, with Joe Pesci,
in the movie "Goodfellas"
Where he thinks he's about to be "made"
By the time he grasps he's going to be whacked
It's too late to be afraid

The Dennis Hotel on the Highway in Frankston
Circa nineteen seventy two
A bit of a trek but I followed the music
What else was a poor boy to do?

The name of the venue, aptly, "King Neptunes"
Fitting in more than one way
It attracted the shallow end of the gene pool
And belonged at the arse of the bay

I arrived nice and early to get a good possie
Near the stage, between PA and walls
I'd been looking forward to this gig all week
"Lobby Loyde and the Coloured Balls"

When I last saw the band, the crowd was pub rockers
A few hippies - the stoned and deranged
When "The Balls" hit the stage with cropped hair and
mullets
I twigged the demographic had changed

The opening chord of, "Hey what's your name?"
And the stage lights lit up the room
For the first time the crowd could see one another
No longer concealed in the gloom

Every Sharpie, every Stylist, every Skinhead in
Melbourne
Filled every square inch of the floor
By my calculation, roughly two thousand
Stood between me and the door

I edged to the wall, avoiding eye contact
I knew I could be seriously hurt
But it's a hard to blend in with a room full of sharps
In flares and pink paisley shirt

A sea of T-shirts, gang names emblazoned
Jeans, too small and pulled high
A culture of violence screamed, "with us or agin us"
I accepted I was going to die

Conte cardigans and pinstripe pants
Cuban heels on all leather shoes
While I contemplated life after death
"The Balls" played "Mess of the Blues"

Assuming I managed to sneak out the exit
There'd be hundreds queued up in the street
They'd be even more agro cause they couldn't get in
And me? Well I'd be dead meat

Lobby's guitar snarled into "Human Being"
Sent the crowd into a juddering trance
Nodding Neanderthals, flexing their arms
What was nicknamed the "Coat Hanger" dance

A half empty glass struck the bridge of my nose
Like I'd been smashed with a bat
A voice through the haze screamed, "Hey poofter,
What you gonna do about that?"

Not a lot, I decided, in a room full of sharps
And every one hated my guts
In a blink I took stock of what mattered the most
Coiled up, protecting my nuts

In the time I had left I farewelled my teeth
There was nowhere to run or take cover
I was saved by the fact, while they all hated me
They passionately despised one another

A Westside Skin hooked a South Blackburn Sharp
The room erupted in rage
In the midst of the brawl a hand grabbed my collar
I was dragged back behind stage

The arm belonged to a Coloured Ball's roadie
The only other bloke with long hair
"You stupid prick," he exclaimed dumfounded
"What the fuck are you doing in there?"

Indebted, I thanked him on behalf of my face
And escaped out the rear loading dock
"The Balls" followed me along Kananook Creek
As they roared into "Liberate Rock"

Bands come and go, and fashions the same
What shines is not always a star
No other sound in this world or the next
Came close to Lobby's guitar

Even today, that song gives me shivers
Lobby, the Balls, R.I.P.
I'm not sure they managed to liberate rock
But they sure helped liberate me

BALLOONS

A west wind whips through Melbourne;
A late spring afternoon
A young boy leaves a party,
Clutching a balloon

Balloons and wind are lovers,
More than young minds understand
A gust reveals its passion;
Tears the treasure from his hand

As it soars into the heavens
Disappointment turns to tears
Wind cares not for sentiment;
The balloon soon disappears

His mother's soothing words
Offer only scant relief
Balloons at best are fickle;
The wind, at best, a thief

Truth cannot yield to hope,
Were even truth to yearn
No balloon, once free,
Was ever tempted to return

BAYS

I suppose, at a pinch,
it could be classified a boat
The fact it reached the beach at all,
proved it could float

Beautifully constructed;
not bothered by the swell
Not exactly ocean going;
still it handled waves quite well

The deck, varnished oak:
the hull, Prussian blue
High above the bow,
embossed, the number sixty two

A little hard to steer
without a rudder or a wheel
Stability was iffy,
but then it didn't have a keel

It was, by any measure,
a superbly fashioned craft
Though we christened it a ship
it was closer to a raft

To those who strode its deck,
a galleon, and more
Though in truth, it should be said,
it was technically - a door!

To parents, yet more rubbish
washed up in Half Moon Bay

Their children, minds less jaded,
saw potential straight away

Like flies around a carcass
they descended on their prize
Excitement in their laughter;
adventure in their eyes

They sailed that piece of flotsam,
beyond both wind and tide
To the edge of their imaginings;
inventiveness their guide

It graced the beach all summer,
to the local kid's delight
Until the first weekend in March,
when it vanished overnight

Carried on the current;
perhaps half way cross the earth?
Or scrapped by those who could not see
its beauty or its worth

Things are cast aside;
objects, people, dreams
Not all is as we see it:
Not all is as it seems

Joy can lie in simple things:
This world can bluff you blind
That's the thing with doors:
you never know what lies behind

BELLS

"Pig" Mills did not hate school;
he just didn't give a stuff
By the time he'd finished kinder,
his brain had had enough

He had few aspirations besides
make each meal a winner
His long term goals extended
about as far as dinner

Still, he did have one ambition
mere eating couldn't quell
Just once, before the year was out,
he'd like to ring the bell

For "Pig" it wasn't honour,
but the power that he'd command
To have the whole school sweating,
like putty in his hand

Last Friday of each month
 a student was selected
Not chosen by the teachers,
by their peers, elected

Usually someone good at netball,
arithmetic or cricket
"Pig" couldn't spell or add
and he'd yet to take a wicket

He wasn't academic,
had no flair for sport or arts

But his skill was without equal
when it came to lighting farts

His dad proudly predicted,
"There's a future there by Jove
A pipe up that boy's clacker
could easily power a stove"

So "Pig" spread the word;
as always, over dramatised
"The Science Lab; lunchtime:
sunglasses advised"

"The stupendous "Piggy" Mills,
will present an exhibition
Of the miracle of body gas
Intesto-rectal fission"

The night before he feasted,
to eliminate all doubts
Two dozen eggs, baked beans
and a box of Brussels sprouts

Next afternoon at half past twelve,
he lay down on the table
A pillow underneath his arse,
helped to keep him stable

Addressed the crowd, flexed his gut,
an in-built butter churner
Instructed "Rabbit", his assistant,
to light the Bunsen burner

Dropped a couple of poppers;
yielding no more than a spark

Ordered "Rabbit" to close the curtains:
it had greater effect in the dark

He attempted to cough up a Roman Candle,
but it petered out near his knees
The punters were restless,
Shouting, "C'mon "Pig" cut the cheese"

A few little high pitched whiners,
good colour but not much smell
Then a shimmering wave of orange blue flame,
"Pig" titled, "The Gates of Hell"

The next resembled a Catherine Wheel:
the sound, like undoing a zip
"Pig" appeared slightly unnerved,
then he really let rip

A blinding flash lit up the room:
the wail of a lonely dog
The lingering glow of a maritime flare
to the horn of a ship in the fog

"Pig" like a pilot in freefall, groaned,
"I think I ate too many eggs"
As a mammoth, unholy, fireball
erupted between his legs

It hung in the air, like a spectre,
and when it seemed about to expire
It rallied, bounced off the ceiling,
setting the curtains on fire

His classmates exited screaming;
and "Pig" could have burned to death

But his methane exhausted the oxygen
and the flames ran out of breath

They hauled "Pig" out to the corridor,
where "Rabbit" attempted first aid
"The bells," moaned "Pig"," I hear the bells?"
Yeah, the bells of the fire brigade

He copped six months of detentions;
but strangely "Pig" wasn't bitter
The thrill of recalling his school mates terror,
put joy into picking up litter

He was destined never to ring the bell;
unlike most in his class
But delighted knowing what required their fingers,
he'd achieved with his arse

BIG AND SMALL

From a tiny seed, a mountain ash
From localized greed, a global crash

Two bullets triggered World War One
Two bullets from a pocket gun

Less than half an ounce of lead
Left more than sixteen million dead

For the price of a bullet, a worthier fight
Fred Hollows gave the gift of sight

Despite the carnage of the Somme
Every bullet, every bomb

No giant cannon, ever lit
Can match a single atom, split

For size, alone, does not reflect
Potential, influence, effect

One word can spark a revolution
Incite division or resolution

A solitary word or act
Can bind, awaken, spur, attract

Drops form rivers, notes build chords
Armies gauged by guns and swords

Bricks make walls and peasants, kings
The world is turned by butterfly wings

BLUE EYES

She was warned the journey was dangerous
Trouble may lie ahead
She had the choice to turn back then
But chose to continue instead

They spoke a language strange to her
Words she did not understand
The uncertainty all travellers feel
In a foreign, lawless land

She wasn't sure who to trust
There were serious drugs involved
Considering what she stood to gain
For the moment, her fears dissolved

Till she found herself surrounded
A gang of six or more
Their faces masked, their eyes intense
She felt her heart rate soar

The ambush caught her by surprise
No time to be afraid
Distracted by the chaos
She didn't even feel the blade

Drawn toward a golden light
Calm and rapture grew
A pair of eyes shone through the glow
Incandescent blue

"Are these the eyes of God?" she thought
Like sapphires set in pearl

A reassuring voice announced
"A healthy five-pound girl"

BRASS

"Pig" Mills surveyed the notice board
And mumbled, deep in thought,
"No experience necessary
Volunteers are sought"

"Volunteers?" snarled "Rabbit"
"Volunteers for what?"
"Pig" paid no attention
He was onto something hot

Their school was the recipient
Of a significant donation
An inheritance bequeathed
With a single stipulation

A percentage must be set aside
The solitary demand
To establish and maintain
A military brass band

"Pig" had no love of music
No interest and no ear
So it came as some surprise
He was first to volunteer

In terms of pure IQ
His brain was more like spam
But akin to Albert Einstein
At sniffing out a scam

He was quick to see the benefits
Supporting his decision

Three hours off school, twice a week
With zero supervision

If the band rehearsed or not
The school didn't give a damn
They'd met their obligations
The money in the can

Built a dedicated band room
Beyond the football ground
They named that tin shed "Canberra"
Not a living thing around

The music teacher, Mr Sloak
Shared their cosy club
He'd open up the room for them
Then nick off to the pub

"Squirrel" chose the tenor horn
"Rabbit" baritone
Lindy Dent the coronet
Bruno, slide trombone

"Pig" selected tuba
To everyone's surprise
Given he loathed lifting
And the tuba's weight and size

At the first so called "rehearsal"
"Pig's" reasons were revealed
That tuba was a Trojan horse
Its true purpose concealed

Five cans of "Frosty" Lemonade
Were stashed inside the bell

Two large bags of "Freckles"
"Sherbet Bombs" as well

Half a dozen "Musk Sticks"
His Dad's "Man" Magazine
"Snowballs", "All Day Suckers"
And a pack of "Capstan Green"

Their scam may have lasted
Had "Pig" chosen not to gloat
"The only band" he boasted,
"That's never played a note"

If he'd only kept his mouth shut
But word soon got about
The board didn't give a stuff
But didn't want it getting out

They called a snap inspection
At the Principal's behest
A performance to judge
How the students had progressed

Regrettably for "Pig"
They chose the worst time of the day
The rest had nicked off early
To share a "Craven A"

It was up to "Pig" to fly the flag
He stood up gingerly
"The tuba only has three valves
How hard can it be?"

You have to give him credit
He was prepared to have a go

Pity he took half an hour
To work out where to blow

He licked, then pursed his lips
Blew for all that he was worth
His cheeks bulged then contracted
Like a hippo giving birth

From the tuba – not a sound
Not a peep for all his strain
"Pig" fell back exhausted
Prepared to try again

The Principal looked down the bell
As "Pig" Mills gave his all
A frozen "Sunny Boy" shot out
Near knocked him through the wall

When the old boy came to
Ten stitches in his crown
"Pig" was caned, the tuba crushed
The school brass band stood down

There's a lesson in this sorry tale
Musicians should take heed
Especially guitarists
Playing more notes than they need

A smoking riff has its place
Though it pays to be selective
As "Pig" Mills demonstrated
Sometimes one note's more effective

BOATS

A hike across the coastal hills,
weaved west towards the shore
A trek to purge the many sins
indulged the night before

A village; picture perfect,
nestled tight beside the loch
An old wooden dory,
sitting idly in dry dock

A fisherman; face weathered,
carved by sea and salt
His forehead cleaved and furrowed,
akin the Great Glen fault

A coat of Prussian blue,
plied carefully to the hull
Overseen, in silence,
by a lone Atlantic gull

"Beautiful boat," I offered,
knowing nought of what I spoke
He turned, eyebrow raised,
as though I'd told a tasteless joke

"A beauty? Aye," he smirked
"if you judge by paint and tar
But it's fishes you'd be joining
if you tried to cross the bar"

"In its day it earned its keep,
but its day has gone for good

It's paint you'd be admiring;
it's thicker than the wood"

"A lawyer pays me handsomely
to keep this tub afloat
It rarely tastes the water;
more trophy than a boat"

"Two homes remain in local hands;
the rich have claimed the rest
They drive up from the south,
a month a year at best"

"They buy here for the atmosphere,
then rob it of its soul
Our children forced to leave,
lost to cities and the dole"

"This place is like a ghost town
eleven months a year
We lost our shop and pub;
thirty miles to share a beer:

"Claimed our history and culture:
those remaining deemed as quaint
Illusion helped by fools like me,
daubing skeletons with paint"

Money tore this place apart
Restored the body, stilled the heart
The winds blow fierce and clouds float by
Gulls, they scavenge and boats stand dry

CUP

Banks are renowned for fleecing
Most Telecoms as well
But the airport leaves them all for dead
As a thieving, exploitive, cartel

A simple cup of tea, that's all
Hard to stuff that up
A tea bag and hot water
In a flimsy paper cup

I don't take milk or sugar
How much could they ask?
"You're kidding me, six dollars!
You crooks should wear a mask"

I told them they're no different
Than a bandit with a gun
Analogies to firearms
Not the smartest thing I've done

Security arrived
As I screamed out, "It's a con"
Baffled by my accent
They thought I'd yelled out "bomb"

What happened next is hazy
My neck's still in a brace
I can't recall which I preferred
The stun gun or the mace

Still, everything's been sorted out
Which comes as some relief

Just one more operation
To free the tea bag from my teeth

The weather's nice in Lisbon
As far as I can tell
A constant forty eight degrees
Down here in my cell

My Portuguese, improving
Which is just as well I'm told
Cause it's all I'll here for five years
When I'm due to be paroled

A cup of cha three times a day
What's more, provided free
The lengths you have to go
For a bloody cup of tea

DAISY

Drinkers at The Bear,
were a straightforward, crusty lot
Council workers mostly;
what you saw was what you got

If you tried spinning bullshit
you didn't stand a chance
Even brown bread on your sandwich
would earn a sideways glance

But everyone liked Daisy,
though none had seen her face
They'd hear her, usually evenings,
as she strolled about the place

That Daisy was accepted,
was surprising all the more
Given Daisy died, allegedly,
two centuries before

It started out as creaking,
then footsteps in the hall
The gaffer woke one night
to someone banging on the wall

When he turned the lights on
there was no-one in the room
He swore he smelt an odour,
like the scent of cheap perfume

One evening after closing,
he was stacking up the chairs

He clearly heard the sound of someone
coming down the stairs

Clunking down the corridor,
like a dragging chain
Once again he searched;
once again in vain

Rose drank at The Bear,
a librarian, retired
The chance to do some digging
soon had her interest fired

She trawled the Parish Records;
left not a stone unturned
Even hard-nosed sceptics
were amazed by what she learned

In the early eighteen hundreds,
the landlord died, alas
Tapping barrels in the cellar,
he was overcome by gas

His wife, whose name was Daisy,
overwhelmed by grief and dread
Died, not two months later,
of a broken heart it's said

A newspaper account,
years after the affair
Tells of supernatural incidents
occurring at The Bear

Noises, apparitions,
objects moving back and forward

Perhaps Daisy's ghost searching
for the husband she adored

The mystery had been solved,
or so it seemed at first
Till the toilets overflowed
when the aging sewer burst

The plumber replaced every S-bend,
pipe and drain
From that day forth, Daisy's ghost
was never heard again

The regulars were forced
to reluctantly admit
The tale of Daisy's ghost
was just a pile of shit

DARLING

Please don't call me "Darling."
I find it really grating
Like nails scraped down a blackboard:
God, it's nauseating

> Well I have to call you something.
> "Hey you" sounds pretty lame

Here's something novel.
You could call me by my name

> But "Ian" sounds so wet!
> Especially paired with "Bland"
> And in that flannel shirt, I mean,
> Oh, you wouldn't understand

I understand precisely,
You're so "upper middle class"
Your problem, like your friends,
Is your heads stuck up your...

> Look, it's meant to be affectionate;
> Not a word you'd comprehend
> After twenty years
> You still introduce me as "your friend"

Well you are my friend
But I don't call you "Babe" "Doll" or "Honey"
How should I introduce you?
My cuddly little bunny?

Look, "Darling" is endearing:
It's warm, romantic, tender
Which you think means a steak
That's been softened in a blender

See this, my passport, "Ian Bland"
Agreed, you wouldn't choose it
But good or bad, I'm stuck with it,
So why not simply use it?

So what if "Darling's" not your name?
What is there to hate?
When we go down the pub
You call everybody "mate"

That's completely different.

Yeah, hypocritical for one thing

You know I can't remember names,
I have to call them something

"Darling's" so pretentious,
It stinks like cheap perfume
Like some shallow, petty, socialite,
Swanning round the room

It's demeaning, affectatious,
Rude and patronising
Which from someone with your intellect,
I frankly find surprising

You pompous, two faced, tosser.
Are your talents never ending?
Decrying patronising

With a serve of condescending

Your poetry or your bigotry.
I'm not sure which is worse
You know behind your back
You're called the Forrest Gump of verse

Forrest who?
Just please don't call me "Darling"
Especially in company, no maybes, ifs or buts

Alright, alright, you've made your point.
Relax, I won't forget
I will never, ever, call you darling, ever!
Okay pet?

Yeah, that's much better,
Alright then – Hey, hang on!

DEEP

She said "You're a really nice bloke;
really nice – really
I like you a lot.
I mean that – sincerely"

"With the right person,
the right chemistry"
I thought, God, here it comes,
"It's not you, it's me"

Instead she uttered,
"It's not me, it's you"
I thought, "Is she trying to tell me
we're through?"

"Something is missing,
don't take offence
I need someone deeper,
more passionate, intense"

Well, I did get upset –
frankly quite mad
"The footy was on –
"Can't this wait till an ad?"

My response, I realise,
was lacking in tact
But my passion made up
for the insight it lacked

"I can do deep
if it stops you from goin'

Watch "Days of our lives"
and play Leonard Cohen"

"I've read Aristotle:
well, some bits I missed
So I just read the cover –
but I got the gist"

"My interests run deep:
I'm into the arts
Manet and Monet
and all those dead farts"

She called me a philistine:
claimed I was strange
I begged, "Wait till the game ends,
I promise I'll change"

She wasn't convinced:
I could tell by the pause
My old Baywatch t-shirt
wasn't helping my cause

I'd make one last effort:
something romantic
Entertainment or culture?
Let's not get pedantic

I considered the ballet,
the theatre and dinner
Then, inspiration;
I came up with a winner

Gold reserved seats;
the only two left

A mud wrestling contest –
fight to the death

I don't think she liked it:
I'm not really sure
Took off in a cab
leaving me at the door

I mean, how deep is deep?
Mud up to your knees?
I guess some people
are too hard to please

DIXIE (JOHN KENNEDY)

Prior to World War Two
he was a missionary priest
The devil and man's cruelty,
not so different a beast

Whether savages or soldiers,
saving souls, his stock and trade
He enlisted, as a chaplain,
in the 23rd Brigade

Sailed from Darwin up to Timor
in December forty one
Surrendered two months later
but his fight had just begun

The records list him missing,
though very much alive
Then a blank, till liberation,
in September forty five

No mention of his journey:
the resilience and fears
The brutality and hardships
that filled those missing years

Traumatised and troubled
by all the things he saw
He could not resume his calling
on returning from the war

Retiring to a cottage
in the monastery grounds

He withdrew from public life,
seeking peace in his surrounds

He tended to the gardens
and laboured on the farm
After all he must have witnessed
he deserved a life of calm

Amongst his few possessions
when he died aged eighty two
A keepsake of his years
as a P.O.W.

A mess tin, a "Dixie":
part of every soldier's kit
In itself, nothing special:
it was what was done to it

He'd engraved on every surface:
with what, we'll never know
A log of all the years
the records did not show

Java, to Changi,
Formosa to Japan
The Burma Thailand Railway,
Manilla and Pusan

Finally, Manchuria,
till eventually set free
A journey thousands started:
a day many would not see

Meticulously entered, though his tools,
no doubt, were crude

His "Dixie" ripe for etchings:
it saw so little food

I wonder, as he etched,
if it ever crossed his mind
This tin might be his epitaph,
all he left behind

In appalling conditions
he found a way to cope
Armies' march on stomachs:
Faith survives on hope

DUST (DORRIE PURVIS)

The smallest speck of dust
had Dorrie Purvis in a fluster
Felt nude without her rubber gloves
and trusty feather duster

Rain or shine, Dorrie
rose at six o'clock each morn
Cleaned the stove, while husband Sid,
prepared to mow the lawn

Everyday she'd go to war
with scrubbing brush and broom
Wax and buff the lino,
then, vacuum every room

Burnish and shine the fondue set,
soak the towels in bleach
Brush the chenille curtains,
and iron them, two times each

Comb the shag pile carpet,
lay each strand left to right
Polish all the silver;
only time it saw the light

Swab the mauve venetian blinds,
rinse and dry each slat
Disinfect the telephone,
shake the sea-grass mat

Sanitise the doilies,
scrape underneath the fridge

Plump the velvet cushions,
embroidered with the Harbour Bridge

Dust the flying ducks;
give the braided rug a beating
Inspect the couch for dandruff
then replace the plastic sheeting

The bathroom was her palace,
she tended it with pride
No whiskers in this basin,
Dorrie made Sid shave outside

Though visitors were welcome,
none ever used the toilet
Bodily functions,
Dorrie felt would only spoil it

Meanwhile, in the garden,
Sid cleared cobwebs, under eaves
Strung netting round the shrubs
to capture falling leaves

Round each bush, a car tyre;
painted high gloss white
A six foot concrete brolga,
concealed the front yard light

Daily Sid mowed the lawn,
which neighbours thought a farce
Since all, except the nature strip,
was artificial grass

He cleaned the Zephyr every day,
as often as the stove

This seemed a trifle odd
as neither Sid nor Dorrie drove

One arvo Dorrie noticed
the bathroom door was locked
Paced up and down the hallway,
cleared her throat and knocked

No response, she quickly tired
of trying to be discreet
She yelled, "Sid, remember,
your arse is not to touch the seat"

Still no reply from Sid,
and Dorrie busting for a pee
Placed a clothes peg on her nose
and went and grabbed the key

Sid was perched bolt upright-dead;
wide eyed as Ginger Meggs
Dorrie, bladder bursting,
had to pee between his legs

It seems poor Sid had died
while doing crosswords in the loo
Dorrie mopped around him;
what else was she to do?

When the undertakers knocked
Dorrie stopped them at the door
Made them take their shoes off
so they wouldn't scuff the floor

The funeral was a quiet affair;
the church was small, but neat

Dorrie greeted mourners
and made sure they wiped their feet

The casket, clad with Laminex;
Dorrie was insistent
Stylish, tough, but best of all,
dirt and stain resistant

Only at the graveside
did Dorrie lose control
"I'm worried 'bout the muck"
she sobbed, "Not his bloody soul"

So Sid returned to whence he came;
as do we all, in time
Illusion is a thin veneer
and can't expunge the grime

For leaves will fall, paint will peal,
cars will yield to rust
Despite our grand pretences,
the world is nought, but dust

EASY

"Easy to install":
words I like to hear
Emblazoned across the brochure;
positive and clear

Despite Luddite inclinations
I admit I felt inspired
I didn't see the asterisk:
"*Assembly Required"

Though I don't believe in hell,
if I did, then my idea
Would be spending all eternity
trapped inside IKEA

"Easy" is subjective
and depends to whom you're talking
It might well be for Einstein,
Marie Curie, Stephen Hawking

Once marketing takes over,
the truth, let's say, gets blurred
"Easy" was stretching it,
"Impossible" is the word!

While I'm not exactly useless
I could be if I tried
Whoever wrote that brochure,
I'm not shy to say they lied

I opened up the box
and carefully studied the directions

And another ten page booklet,
simply titled "Corrections"

All dreams of "easy" vanished
when I found a plastic packet
Ambihelical Hexnuts?
Rectangular Excrusion Bracket?

I suspected this was going
to take longer than I thought
What in hell's
a Trichotometric Indicator Support?

I laid every panel neatly,
in order on the floor
It promised sixty lag screws,
but there were only fifty four

Still, better than the button heads,
for fastening the struts
They'd included fifteen extras
but forgot the jam lock nuts?

If I was versed in Mandarin
it may have been a breeze
Something went awry
when translated from Chinese

"Place A on top of B inside,
being careful not being stain
Push upwards to the downwards;
more could causing strain"

"Turn clockwise to the left,
should it wanting to the right

Remove only this at random,
letting go, holding tight"

"Human Cutter, slicing one ways,
being much supported
Do not stick knife in children"
Glad we got that sorted

"Put ring protecting fingers
on top side going under
Hiding screw must be visible,
inserting not to sunder"

"Adapt to matching ear part;
watching turning through
Abide by drawing circled,
snapping closely, that be do"

"Not good, only better;
trying this to easy find
Doing this way, not other way,
do not change it on your mind"

"All can available,
not with problems only bolts
Bring forwards, where to started,
happy to like faults"

Well it took me fifteen hours
but I eventually succeeded
I dispensed with plans and spanners;
frankly they weren't needed

It gave me satisfaction,
despite the subtlety it lacks

Where I failed with an Allen key
I triumphed with an axe

I chopped it into pieces;
tiny scraps of wood
It voided my warranty
but didn't it feel good?

I jammed it in the bin;
every grommet, strut and screw
I can't even recall
what that thing was supposed to do

But I kept the instructions,
they're still somewhere about
At times, when life gets crazy,
I pull that manual out

It points me to the forest
when I'm obsessing on the tree
Easy's sometimes harder
than even harder needs to be

ELWOOD

I was born in Elwood
Where Addison meets Shelley
Henry Bolte ruled the state
Zig and Zag, the telly

Rock'n'roll, as new
As the Dibbs' green FJ
Elvis had his blue suede shoes
We had Doris Day

Dad caught the bus to work
Less crowded than the tram
While mum stacked the shopping
All around me in the pram

We'd amble home down Broadway
In time to get me fed
Jammed between a bag of spuds
And half loaf of bread

If the weather was convivial
We'd do the Tour Royale
A stroll around Point Ormond
Then along the old canal

Alf and Dulcie Cornish
Lived upstairs in number four
Miss Caruthers and her sister
Taught piano right next door

Across the road, the Rowswells
Held by all in high regard

It was there, one Sunday afternoon
I saw my first backyard

An affable politeness
Like a gentle autumn breeze
Doors were always open
Children were the keys

The legacy of war
Though tacit, still survived
In kids they saw renewal
Innocence, revived

Bert Jones, retired accountant
If nothing else, was willing
He opened me a bank account
Deposited a shilling

"Compound interest, watch it grow"
He wisely told my Mum
"When the lad turns eighteen
He should have a tidy sum"

Our little flat was big enough
For Mum and Dad and me
But when my sister gate-crashed
It felt cramped with more than three

Dad promised us one day
We'd have a mortgage of our own
Mum whipped up a meatloaf
The day we got the loan

We said goodbye to Elwood
And our cosy little box

Headed to the suburbs
And the quarter acre blocks

The day I turned eighteen
It was Bert I had to thank
Cause the bus fare cost me more
Than awaited in the bank

FARM

It was eggs that tipped him over the edge –
scrambled – or so they claimed
Henry reckoned serving that sludge –
well, the chickens were being defamed

We're the oddest of creatures-more than we grasp –
odd without even knowing
We take the worst that life dishes up
and find a way to keep going

Then a seemingly insignificant thing
and we'll snap, brought to our knees
Like a tree that endures a cyclone,
then falls to a hint of a breeze

In the six months he'd lived in the nursing home,
Henry seemed happy and calm
The previous eighty seven years,
Henry's life was his farm

His grandparents settled in the late 1800's –
cleared every acre by hand
Henry was born on the living room table –
all he'd known was that land

He met his wife Dulce at a public meeting
on controlling Patterson's Curse
Despite a face described as a sheep's arse with
eyebrows,
Dulce took him for better or worse

What with droughts, fires, rabbits and locusts it seemed
she'd copped more of the latter
But potential suitors were rarer than bunyips –
and looks – well they didn't matter

Her mother and father met at a meeting
to eradicate Prickly Pear
Besides, Dulce was tired of going to funerals
and hoping to meet someone there

She was left to manage the farm for a time
while Henry went off to war
The day he came home he went straight to the shed
to finish sharpening his saw

The New Guinea jungles had taken their toll
but work round the farm couldn't wait
"That's enough travelling for me" Henry vowed –
and he never again left the state

A week on the coast every year was for Dulce;
to Henry it didn't make sense
I mean why would want to lie on a beach
when you could be mending a fence?

Breakfast; two eggs, at five every morning
with the prize winning sauce Dulcie made
"So fresh they were poached," Henry observed
"Before the chooks even knew they'd been laid"

Both of them desperately wanted a family,
but it wasn't destined to be
Henry made light, "It's probably best –
might of ended up looking like me"

No time for self pity; not on a farm:
though in private they shed a few tears
Instead they reared calves and Dulcie raised chickens:
together for fifty two years

They were down by the creek with harness and
chains-
a heifer had got itself stuck
Henry, digging it free from the mud,
while Dulce gently pulled with the truck

He gave her a wave to take up the strain,
the engine revved hard, then went dead
He found Dulcie slumped, hands on the wheel –
"Her heart", the doctor said

Fifty two years, gone, in a heartbeat;
he struggled once Dulcie was gone
But there was always something that needed doing
and Henry muddled along

Locals noticed a steady decline –
the paddocks covered in weeds
Fences broken; stock on the road,
with little water or feed

One Sunday morning the kettle boiled dry
and the kitchen nearly burnt down
The authorities ordered Henry assessed,
he was moved to a care home in town

From a ten minute drive to his closest neighbour
to a stranger sharing his room
He didn't complain, appeared quite content:
at least that's what they assumed

So the scrambled eggs caught them by surprise;
the doctor recommended sedation
They failed to grasp there's a difference
between contentment and resignation

The nurse, at least, proved observant
and more insightful than most
"Give Henry a spanner and something to fix —
and for breakfast, just give him toast"

They found him some tools, things settled down,
no more of Henry's tirades
He spent his days in the maintenance shed,
repairing mobility aids

We're all of us quirky, each in our way,
even when on our last legs
Perhaps we don't always know what we want —
but we know how we don't want our eggs

FIELDS

The farm house still remained
Though threatening to fall
The paddocks long since swallowed
By the endless urban sprawl

At its peak, three hundred acres
Now whittled down to two
Wedged between the factories
A highway for a view

Lottie Carr was born there
Her family, pioneers
The only home she knew
In her ninety seven years

When Lottie died and left no will
None claimed her estate
The council took possession
In lieu of unpaid rates

That land enticed the local kids
Like moths drawn to a flame
They called it "Lottie's Field"
They were quick to stake their claim

They clambered up the pines
Once the entrance to the farm
Some brought down old motor bikes
The odd spill, but no harm

They sat around a campfire, talking
Sipping smuggled port

A place to test their wings
Without the fear of being caught

A chunk of land un-manicured
Just scrub and rocks and dirt
Not choked by regulations
In case some child is hurt

Kids just being kids
As they fumbled through their teens
It takes a hint of danger
To learn what danger means

But the council flogged the land off
Some chain from overseas
A warehouse ringed by barbed wire
While a car park claimed the trees

Now kids are penned in playgrounds
Dictated by a sign
No ball games, no skateboards
Hundred dollar fine

No dogs allowed, no BBQ's
No imagination
The monkey bars and swings removed
In case of litigation

Economic rationalism
A logic we abuse
As the population rises
It seems the more we lose

Councils keep on growing
Demand a bigger share

Yet they've sold or outsourced everything
You wonder why they're there

Child care and nursing homes
And other assets, lost
Sometimes a wise investment
Isn't measured by the cost

The things that bind communities
Aren't ruled by cost and yield
Every town and suburb
Could do with "Lottie's Field"

FLOWERS

The ocean rears in panic
At the tempest's frenzied roar
Enraged, the angry waves
Fiercely pound the hapless shore

Here nature rules unchallenged
As only nature can
No mercy shown to gamblers
Or the vanities of man

Pitiless and brutal
Exhausts all opposition
Even mountains, cleaved by ice and gales
Worn into submission

Trenches form, where peat is cut
Filled by driving rains
Fanned out, for miles across the bog
Entwined, like swollen veins

The cliff face, bare and weathered
As winds and rain collude
Remorseless, unrelenting
Winter's savage mood

Nestled tight, within the crags
A single stand of gorse
It clings to life, like hope itself
Defying nature's force

Rows of thorns give warning
Keeping predators at bay

While tiny buds bring colour
To this scene of endless grey

Golden flowers, like jewels
Yet, ten thousand times their worth
Beauty lives, where man cannot
Flowers rule the earth

FOUR

Neville was a postman
almost all his working life
Didn't earn a fortune
but it kept him out of strife

One evening in the pub,
primed by several beers
He began to reminisce
about the highlights of those years

Neville's tone grew solemn,
not without a hint of pride
"In the service of the public,
four times I nearly died"

"The first, a truck on Barkly Street;
 Barkly Street and Gray
A difference of opinion
as to who was giving way

A broken arm and collarbone,
bruised ribs and two black eyes
The last attempt at cutting off
a bike that truckie tries

The next, involved a dog
down on Walkers Road in Lara
Not a Rottweiler or Pit Bull,
but a three legged Chihuahua

That runt got caught in my spokes,
threw me head first cross the bars

If the stop sign hadn't stopped me,
the next stop was the cars

My third close call, a parcel,
to a house in Taylors Lakes
Some fruitcake tried to use the mail
to smuggle Carpet Snakes

One escaped, slid down my shorts
and started to explore
A woman kindly gave a hand —
which leads to number four

Her husband found us prostrate
with his wife's hand down my pants
I started to explain to him
but never got the chance

His wife cried, "God, it's moving"
hubby didn't seem amused
He kicked me twice, killed one snake,
the other badly bruised

But it all got sorted out
and I lived to tell the tale
No snake or dog or truck stopped me
delivering the mail

It wasn't cars or animals
that got me in the end
Some bureaucrat nailed me
with one stroke of the pen

After forty years on pushbikes,
I told 'em where to shove their motor

Next thing I was pensioned off,
"In excess of quota"

Old Neville ordered one more beer,
the usual dash of lime
Waved goodbye and left for what
proved the final time

Admiring someone's letterbox,
overly engrossed
He was cleaned up by a bright red van,
you guessed; Australia Post

His coffin, a cardboard box,
"Care of Heaven" the address
His friends chipped in to buy the stamps
and sent him off express

Came back "Return to sender,
no Nevilles living here
Suggest you try in Hades"
but the postage was too dear

So they sent Nev down to sorting
where they had him re-assessed
The Dead Letter Office,
Nev was finally laid to rest

FOREVER

"How long we gonna wait?" barked "Pig"
"Ten minutes" Barry said
"Give him a chance" "Squirrel" sighed,
"Has to wait till his dad's in bed"

Barry had gone to nick cigarettes⁻
and with luck, a bottle of port
Couldn't escape till his dad passed out
he'd be dog food if he was caught

So there they sat on a moonless night,
by the trees that bounded the park
"Pig" Mills, as usual, impatient and edgy —
never did like the dark

Whereas "Squirrel" came to life
with the setting of the sun
Unshackled by the darkness,
his mind was free to run

"Infinity" he whispered,
gazing at the stars
"Hello", sneered "Pig", "Anyone home?
Come in, Earth to Mars"

"Endless space" continued "Squirrel"
"Have you ever wondered why?"
"Get your hand off it" "Pig" replied,
"It's just the bloody sky"

"Eternity" "Rabbit" added,
"Life without an end

It sort of does your head in,
kinda hard to comprehend"

"Pig" grumbled disapprovingly,
this was all too Zen
"Look, there's school, weekends, holidays —
then it all starts again"

Thinking made "Pig" hungry
so he sucked a butterscotch
Then woofed into a Boston Bun,
eyes fixed on his watch

Lindy Dent, a wiz at math,
spoke some sense at last
"If the future is eternal,
then so must be the past"

"Which means," she added thoughtfully,
always keen to share
If my theory is correct,
we're exactly halfway there"

"Pig's" brain went into meltdown,
he broke into a sweat
He snapped "I'm sick of waiting
for a stinking cigarette"

"Stuff this," he cried "I'm off home,
you knob-heads think you're clever
The trouble with eternity
is it bloody takes forever"

FUNERALS

"We come to celebrate a life"
or so the Vicar said
But too much celebrating
was the reason Rex was dead

A dozen eggs for breakfast,
though he only ate the yolk
Washed down with a cocktail
of Tabasco, beer and Coke

He could eat three family pizzas
and a double serve of chips
With a cigarette dangling
from the corner of his lips

He wasn't very sociable,
except when after money
Exercise for Rex
was the bedroom to the dunny

Laid out in his coffin
in someone else's Sunday best
The first time, most attending,
had seen Rex fully dressed

Ethel Tonks remarked,
she'd never seen him look so neat
"Though a shame," she lamented,
"Only thongs to grace his feet"

"He looks so slim," sobbed Lorna Glick,
holding back the tears

"The healthiest Rex has looked
for nigh on forty years"

"Healthy?" laughed Col Fibbs,
"He's clearly past his peak.
As for slimmer, don't forget,
he's not eaten for a week"

"You can still smell the alcohol"
Raelene Pickles sighed
The Vicar informed her
it was in fact Formaldehyde

'Formaldehyde? Sounds Greek," she chirped,
"Don't mind a foreign drop
I'll grab a cask on Monday
when I pass the bottle shop"

Frank Peebles gave the eulogy
he'd known Rex since his youth
An entertaining speech
containing not one grain of truth

Not a man of many words,
in fact not a man of one
Frank stole Ted Whitten's eulogy
verbatim from "The Sun"

He might have got away with it:
they'd all had a few grogs
But they cracked up when he claimed
Rex, Captain Coached the Dogs

Sid Shinners lived next door to Rex;
knew him all his life

Having offered her his sympathy,
came on to Rex's wife

"You brazen swine," huffed Agnes Shultz
"The body not yet cold
Peg doesn't need your wayward hands
she needs to be consoled"

"Don't get your undies in a twist,"
Sid retaliated
"I've been consoling Peg for years,
I can wait till he's cremated"

It wouldn't be a funeral
Without Prue Quigley's "Pigs' Foot Pies"
"It's a pity," growled Len Sharp
"We have to wait till someone dies"

He could buy them at Prue's Deli
but Len was tighter than a clam
Even tighter than the lid
On Eunice Biggley's Cumquat jam

Things were loosening up
and the mood was more than merry
The beer supply exhausted
they were drinking pots of sherry

Kevin Bean was telling jokes
and had them on the floor
No-one noticed Sid and Peg
slip quietly out the door

Len pontificated
as he toyed with his moustache

"You know a wedding or a funeral;
I'd take a funeral in a flash"

"There's nothing like a send off,"
Len waxed effervescent
"You don't need an invitation
and they don't expect a present"

The Vicar nodded wryly
"I can tell you this as well
At a funeral you find
a better class of clientele"

"I wonder who'll be next"?
salivated Byron Young
The taste of Prue's Pig Pie
still dancing on his tongue

It was left to Winnie Mears
to have the final word
"That's the end of Rex, I s'ppose:
you know, I thought he was a turd"

GEORGIA'S GARDEN

The garden, long neglected,
bound and overgrown
My shovel glanced a rock, I thought,
a rusted bolt or stone

I broke away a clod of clay
and scraped the sticky mess
No bottle top or shard of glass —
a golden ring no less

Once I'd washed it clean
I found inside the band
Engraved, "Dearest Georgia,
Love Eternally, Stan"

It seemed a good excuse
to put the tools back in the shed
I cracked a beer and pondered
how it found my garden bed

A relationship gone wrong, perhaps?
It wouldn't be the first
Thrown away in anger,
like the love affair, now cursed

Was Georgia once a gardener?
Someone must have been
As her fingers worked the soil
had it fallen off unseen?

Was it pawned to feed the family?
Was it sold to pay the rent?

Was it grieved or soon forgotten?
Cast out or accident?

Had it lain there for a decade,
a century or more?
A soldier's parting gift
as he headed off to war?

Could Georgia still be living
or long gone, as one supposes?
Was this ring spread with her ashes
to dwell amongst the roses?

There was no way of telling,
but I knew, at least, one thing
If only for a moment
great love flowed through this ring

Now I'm no sentimentalist,
quite opposite I'm told
But the value of this ring
once far outweighed the gold

I, for all my wonderings
can never know its worth
I finished off my beer
and dug it back into the earth

No purely selfless act
I admit with no regret
My long neglected garden
needs all the love it can get

GOING BACK

In the grass, beside a track,
a pair of kangaroos
Sensing company, upwind,
they hastily retreat
The silence, briefly hijacked
by a gang of cockatoos
The landscape warps and shimmers
in the unrelenting heat

A car rests, in a clearing,
down a dusty, country lane
A spindly, twisted Grey Box
provides modest shade, of sorts
A woman sits quietly,
gazing out across the plain
Less absorbed in scenery
than her memories and her thoughts

Born here; on this block:
the first time she's been back
Since the night she took flight,
near fifty years before
Ushered by her mother,
they crept in darkness up the track
Her father, drunk as usual
and unconscious on the floor

Five terrifying miles they ran:
Her mother bruised and bleeding
To the sanctuary of neighbours,
then an Auntie's, in Ballan
All these decades on,

she still hears her mother pleading
As that bastard made her pay
for his failures as a man

Hounded by the bank,
little cash for stock or food
But enough to buy whisky
to hold reality at bay
Little knowledge of the land:
anger cloaked ineptitude
A farm too small and barren
to ever pay its way

The complexities of farm life
well beyond his expectation
The freedom he imagined
began to tighten like a noose
Those who should be dearest
bore the brunt of his frustration
A shameful explanation
and it offers no excuse

She remembers sleepless nights
hiding underneath the cover
Terrified he'd beat her
for some imagined sin
The cold, resentful taunt
"You're as useless as your mother"
As he hit her with the phone book
so it wouldn't bruise the skin

Now the scrub's reclaimed the paddocks,
erasing even fences
Bar a strand of rusted wire bound
to blackened shards of wood

The scraggly, thirsty, mulga strips this land
of all pretences
Not a sheet of iron or stump to say
a house had ever stood

A plume of dust roars eastwards,
as though the ground itself is torn
A car recalls the path the night
a child and mother ran
This land of bitter memories may be
the place where she was born
But the night they stole away
was the night her life began

She hasn't come in homage
to mark her place of birth
But to honour a passage
and a mother who was brave
Fear once gnarled these trees
and sucked life from the earth
This place, once her cradle
could have easily been her grave

LETTER

Dear Sir or Madam – whoever you are
Your gender wasn't stated
I suspect you're not even human
But computer generated

Still, thanks for your letter, a source of amusement
As always, a joy to receive
It's filed with the others – straight in the bin
I'm not sure what you hoped to achieve

This brings up your hundred – not that I'm counting
No-one can say you aren't trying
And just as I've done with the last ninety nine
I'm showing courtesy by replying

I realise you're owed nearly Two Hundred Dollars
I can imagine it causes distress
But I've told you before my Uncle Bruce
No longer shares this address

You could ask him yourself – now there's an idea
I'm certain Bruce would be flattered
You'll find him at high tide on Mentone Beach
At least that's where his ashes were scattered

He's as dead, as Monty Python's Parrot
Departed two years as of June
His name's Bruce, you cretins, Bruce, not Lazarus

So no – I'm not expecting him soon
Still, I have to admire your persistence
An outstanding debt really galls

But you gormless primates have blown triple that
Just in postage and calls

That lovely young man you keep sending around
The one with the garlic breath
Personality bypass, wears a black shirt
Demanding some "Proof of death"

Debt Recovery, I think, was his title
"Grunt" I believe was his name
I invited him to screw himself
I suggest you consider the same

Now you're threatening legal action
Brilliant – try suing a ghost
You could serve the summons by Ouija board
It will save a fortune in post

I suggest your minnow brained lawyers
Should stick to ambulance chasin'
Employ mediums to make contact
Try channelling Perry Mason

He's dead you morons, like VHS
Deceased – not hibernating
Do you really think he gives two shits
That he's damaged his credit rating?

Bruce donated his kidneys and liver
And the rest of his organs in turn
If I'd known I'd have saved you his brain you clowns
But all we have left is the urn

His heart gave a woman a second chance
His corneas, sight to two men

Why don't your bloodhounds try sniffing them out?
Get your money, pro rata, from them

His only possession was a budgie named 'Feathers'
Not sure of its sex or its age
Maybe you leeches could flog it on eBay
In the meantime, you clean out its cage

Yours Sincerely, Etcetera, Etcetera
Signed on behalf of the debtor
P.S. take off your clothes and touch your toes
'Cause that's where I'm sending this letter

MANACUNNA

The town of Manacunna,
in the far west of the state
Had, outside of football,
little cause to celebrate

The Manacunna Emus,
coached by Alby Shanks, the Mayor
The players, like their namesake,
next to useless in the air

While they hadn't won a flag
for nye on fifty years
They did have Clarrie Beadle,
revered by all his peers

Over sixty years of age,
a farmer and a vet
Nearly seven hundred games –
and he was wasn't finished yet

One record still eluded,
he was running out of time
First to kick a thousand goals –
he was stuck on nine, nine, nine

Carting hay one arvo
at the far end of his block
He left the engine running
while he went to move some stock

His tractor jumped a gear,
pinning Clarrie to a tree

While lucky to survive,
he lost his leg, above the knee

And that, the town assumed,
was the end of his campaigning
But barely twelve months later
Clarrie fronted up to training

An artificial leg
knocked together in his shed
A spring from an old Bedford
and a foot from his brass bed

Screwed onto a football boot,
the largest ever seen
Size eight and a half! His good foot-
his left, size seventeen

Anybody else,
you'd have thought it was a joke
But no-one doubted Clarrie —
he was not that sort of bloke

They had no heart to tell him
since the abattoir closed down
The club was close to folding,
half the players had left town

The trainer, Tassie Gooch,
"Bugger this," he said
"We've weathered droughts and politics,
we're down, not bloody dead"

"We might have lost some players
but we haven't lost our soul

I, for one, aren't budging
till Clarrie kicks that goal"

Tassie's speech inspired
Old Ernie Dibbs to have a run
Last time he put his hand up
was to serve in World War One

Father Brian, the local priest,
and Cecil Crabbe, the baker
Even Vincent Cafarella,
the local undertaker

Des Gillot used a cane
since diabetes took his sight
"Just point me west" he shouted
"I can still tell day from night"

Tassie's girlfriend Olga,
as tough as hardened steel
A boner at the abattoirs,
she volunteered with zeal

The coach recoiled
"A-a-a-a woman? It's not allowed, fair go"
Olga winked, then whispered
"Relax, no-one will know"

"Give my hair a trim
and flatten out my quiff
And then if I quit shaving,
no-one will know the diff"

Alby stared at Olga's chin,
looking for a trace

"Legs," she snarled "You cheeky prick,
not me bleeding face"
"What about your b- b -bosoms?
They're the size of sacks of wheat
Like trying to hide an elephant,
they hang down to your feet!"

"Calm down Pet" Olga cooed,
"I'll tuck'em in me trunks
It'll look just like a beer gut —
least I'll blend in with you drunks"

So they scraped a team together
to play the Deadfield Tiger Snakes
Never in their history
had they played for higher stakes

Hammered from the opening bounce,
they couldn't take a trick
But they hadn't come to win the game —
just one lousy kick

Clarrie's gait looked awkward,
a bit like Cameron Ling
As he fought to tame the power
of his inbuilt Bedford spring

You wouldn't call it running,
more a skip and then a hop
Speed was not an issue;
His problem? How to stop!

His mechanical appendage thrust him
high above the pack
Ten free kicks he gave away,

all for in the back

Centre to the goal square
took Clarrie just two jumps
But they deemed he'd run too far,
at least according to the umps

Finally, exhausted,
he was forced to seek the bench
Where they massaged Clarrie's leg
with "RP7" and a wrench

As he crawled across the boundary line,
as corny as it sounds
A wit yelled from the terraces
"Look, Clarrie's out of bounds"

With little time remaining,
encouraged by his team
Clarrie came back on
to try to realise his dream

Cecil Crabbe, the baker,
was on a roll and kicked it deep
Clarrie, holding nothing back,
took one gigantic leap

Though it looked spectacular,
his leap was badly timed
Not only did he miss the ball,
he left his leg behind

Olga, thinking quickly,
ripped that leg out of the mud
Charged towards the Sherrin

with a sudden rush of blood

She clubbed the ball as sweetly
as Greg Norman in his prime
Drove it through the middle
as the umpy blew full time

The crowd, lost in silence,
turned as one, towards the ump
While Clarrie kneeled in prayer –
well, one knee and a stump

Even opposition players
willed that pig skin through
But the umpires stood bewildered,
unsure of what to do

Olga broke the impasse, shouting
"Listen here you tools"
And gave them her analysis
of the spirit of the rules

The ball went through the goal,
that was never in dispute
And no-one could deny
it came off Clarrie's boot

They scanned a battered rule book,
every clause dissected
Nothing said your body
and your leg must be connected

So, the umpy blew his whistle,
took a breath and raised his hand
A goal to Clarrie Beadle

Clarrie had his grand

The Grandstand erupted,
a thundering of cheers
Supporters of both teams
stood hugging and in tears

Clarrie had his thousand
and the crowd saw history made
Sadly, that game,
was the last the Emus' played

Lost to all but memory,
in hearts it still survives
Like all the unseen moments
that set apart our lives

Clarrie's gone the way
of his beloved footy club
His boot has pride of place
at the Manacunna Pub

It hangs above the bar
with the rest of Clarrie's kit
Like Cinderella's slipper,
it awaits, the perfect fit

A sign reads "Good home wanted –
wear this if you will,
But a warning to you wannabes –
it's a bloody big boot to fill"

MERCY

My father was ready and wanting to die
A yearning I could not fulfill
The science that bought him a few extra years
Now held him against his will

His body wasted, beyond his control
A mind he could no longer trust
He wandered a half world, confused and tormented
Reason – even memories, mere dust

The God he'd relied on for meaning and guidance
Could seemingly grant no assistance
Not that my father abandoned his faith
He'd forgotten its very existence

His comfort, well being, entrusted to carers
Reliant on their expertise
For that precious task they're paid even less
Than those who repair our TVs'

Those horrible, pitiless, lucid moments
When a drowning man glimpses a boat
His eyes would plead, resigned beyond fear
Run his forefinger over his throat

Would I have the strength or resolve to release him
If given my chances again?
Or count, as I did, on the whimsy of nature
Complicit in his anguish and pain

Instead nurses and doctors must carry that burden
Mercy, unspoken, unseen

Allowing pneumonia to blossom, untreated
And a generous dose of morphine

I respect the beliefs of those who contend
The taking of life is divine
I respect their beliefs but hold with contempt
Those who would disrespect mine

Denied the relief and compassion
We show to a dog or a cat
Prisoners of religion and politics
And I find little mercy in that

ORANGE

Beverly Purvis to the seventies
was chained
While that decade ended long ago,
Beverly remained

Lava lamps, egg chairs,
vibrant and pristine
The décor, a subtle blend of orange
and lime green

Camisoles and hot pants,
high waisted denim flares
Spaghetti strapped tank tops,
orange, like the chairs

A chrome atom chandelier,
bathed the lounge in light
The kitchen, glazed with orange tiles,
not a pastel tone in sight

Once the height of fashion
now horribly outdated
To everyone but Beverly,
the colour scheme now grated

One night in nineteen ninety eight
as Bev took off her choker
She fancied a Virginia Slim:
she'd always been a smoker

While searching for a lighter
in her BoHo crocheted bag

It tangled in the carpet,
an orange, long pile shag

Bev fell onto her fondue set,
the skewers went through her knees
Then headfirst in the dipping pot
and drowned in molten cheese

It was death by misadventure,
the coroner recorded
While the cause was indisputable,
the details were more sordid

Bev hadn't choked on Stilton,
Danish Blue or Brie
It was common processed cheddar:
so nineteen seventy three

Her things went to the Charity Shop,
and in time began to rot
Till a dealer spied them out the back,
paid twenty bucks, the lot

Now he's asking fifteen hundred
for the vinyl bar stools – each
No longer classed as orange,
no, they're Autumn Sunset Peach

The orange velvet pouf
that was such a pig to clean
Is now listed as a "Love Seat",
in Atomic Tangerine

Fashion is a fickle beast,
both arrogant and chaste

We, so insecure,
entrust it with our taste

A hue, once loved, repels
as our sense of judgement falters
It is us who're dull, not colours,
for the rainbow never alters

PEACE

Bent Street in the sixties,
a community at ease
The drone of Victa mowers
like a swarm of worker bees

Mothers at the Hills Hoist
hanging Y-fronts by the load
Kids playing hopscotch
in the middle of the road

A street in perfect harmony:
no friction or pretence
That was until Reg Henshaw
tried to build a new side fence

His neighbour Leonard Crock concurred
the fence could stand replacing
But neither could agree which way
the palings should be facing

"They've always been on our side"
snarled Leonard holding firm
"Exactly," grumbled Reg, with grit
"It's time we had a turn"

Now neither gave a stuff which side
the rail or palings went
It was all about "The principle"
No-one quite knew what that meant

"Toss a coin" sighed Beryl Crock
"Fixed, once and for all"

But they couldn't agree who'd toss
and which of them would call

Things turned really nasty
when the Henshaw's mail was shredded
"Stumpy", their beloved garden gnome
was found next day – beheaded

Beryl Crock's Azallias died
every single blossom
Reg laughed when challenged, smugly sneered
"Must have been a possum"

Then the Henshaw's toilet overflowed,
with Reg still on the seat
Someone filled their sewer vent
with rapid set concrete

The fence, by now in ruins,
grew more shaky by the week
No hope of resolution
since both sides refused to speak

Neighbours tried to mediate
but none could find the answer
Peace began to crumble
as the feud spread like a cancer

The Luccis sued their neighbours,
Paul and Eva Sanchez
For damage to their gutter
caused by overhanging branches

Complaints regarding parties,
parking and the din

The drums at number thirty five,
next door, the violin

Objections re his trumpet forced
Vin Smith to call it quits
So instead he took up bagpipes
to give everyone the shits

There were quarrels over unkempt lawns,
smoke from barbeques
Complaints about the language shrieked
by Rex Pitt's cockatoos

Conflicts over barking dogs,
tree huts, squeaking gates
Caused the council so much grief they warned
they'd raise the rates

A stupid feud, one tiny crack,
enough to sink the ship
And steer their slice of Eden closer
to the Gaza Strip

Multiply their tiny street
by a hundred million more
It's not difficult to see why it's not hard
to start a war

In the end, the fence collapsed,
killing Leonard, instantly
Reg died from a heart attack
trying to pull Len free

A new side fence was never built:
there lies the paradox

'Cause twenty four apartments
now straddle both the blocks

To keep the peace with neighbours
if you aim to build a fence
Remember, wood is crucial
but far less than common sense

PEARLS

Aged ninety five, Elsie Bent,
departed of this earth
A pair of pink pearl earrings,
all she left, of any worth

Her nieces, Gayle and Bronwyn,
had long coveted those pearls
While Elsie had long tired
of being pressured by the girls

She would teach them both a lesson;
though never one to preach
To her nieces' irritation
they were left one earring each

Earrings, as with cufflinks,
are no use unless a pair
Elsie hoped her legacy
would encourage them to share

Alas, the girls' belligerence,
she underestimated
Each, to spite the other,
had one ear amputated

A path, though not intended,
Elsie helped to pave
Forewarning to those who seek
to dictate from the grave

Her executor remarked
on hearing of the news

"I suppose we should be thankful
Elsie didn't leave them shoes"

Earrings shine no brighter
than what lies between the ears
Pearls, to the oyster,
are nothing more than tears

RACING

"The trouble with racing rarely rests with the horse"
According to the Gospel of Jack
"The trouble with racing," he'd say with conviction
"Is the arsehole who sits on its back"

Jack didn't trust jockeys, and didn't trust trainers
In his day he'd been both; in a fashion
He didn't trust bookies, owners or punters
But horses he loved with a passion

He'd grown up around them; his dad was a breaker
Jack followed him into the game
But a fall in his twenties left him near crippled
One arm next to useless, and lame

For the next forty years he scratched out a living
Moving from stable to stud
Stock horses, Quarters; Shetlands to Clydesdales
And those with much hotter blood

He always found work, though his body was broken
His worth in his manner and tongue
An astonishing gift for calming his charges
Even the most highly strung

"When you're breaking a horse there's only one rule
And that rule is sacred," he said
"You don't break its spirit and you don't break its back
You find a way into its head"

"Horses," he stressed "Are no different to humans
They're all individuals for a start

They might have the breeding, the strength and the
legs
It means little if they don't have the heart"

Well into his eighties Jack still loved the track
Every weekend, sunny or wet
Limp down through the yard and back through the
ring
But not once in his life did he bet

"Punters," he scoffed "Are the base of the food chain
Bankrolling the sharks and high flyers
Those who claim to make a living from punting
Are thieves, deluded or liars"

"I watch these young fellas who think they know
horses
The carry on when they win
Like a bunch of monkeys chasing a peanut
Sucked in by the image and spin"

"You need to remember, where money's involved
The temptation's there to abuse
For every horse saddled to win
There's another been saddled to lose"

"I can pick a good horse," he'd state without ego
"And not by its gait or its size"
"A good horse," he'd chuckle "Will tell you itself,
It's all in the coat and the eyes"

Jack never precisely explained what to look for
"The eyes" was all he would say
If he had, by now I'd be sunning my buns
On a beach up near Byron Bay

Sadly, Jack is no longer with us
His end both ironic and bizarre
Knocked down shuffling home from the races
A jockey was driving the car

ROLL

Egmont Cass the third,
known as "Eggie" to his friends
Departed prematurely,
met the stickiest of ends

A baker by profession,
but a warning to the wise
Very little meat
found its way into his pies

His baking skills were first-rate,
according to reports
But "Eggie" was tighter
than Warwick Capper's shorts

Ground up bone and rind
filled his famous "Bacon Butty"
His pasties, pumped with lard,
the consistency of putty

Gristle, skin and fat
served as "Eggie's" rib eye waffle
His sausage rolls a blend
of stale bread, crumbs and offal

The sign outside the shop,
like his pastries, rather droll
"'Eggie' Cass, Baker –
always on a roll"

A man of contradictions,
and hard to get to know

On one hand he was frugal,
always careful with his dough

But the darker side of "Eggie"
was one you'd not forget
More than partial to a drink
and by God he loved to bet

Horses, blackjack, bingo:
even two flies on a wall
And those bloody awful pokies,
where you have no chance at all

"I'm on a roll" he'd cry,
addicted to the thrill
He was on a roll alright,
but the roll was all down hill

Each loss would fuel another bet:
each bet another drink
Till his pies were nought but sinew
mixed with saw dust in the sink

Plagued by debt,
"Eggie" grew more desperate and meaner
If possible, his pies and sausage rolls
grew even leaner

Till one night, at the football club,
last coin in the machine
The barman shouted hoarsely,
"D 57 Green"

"That's me," yelled Eggie, "Luck has turned,
I said it would, you fools"

"Mate, it's just the meat tray raffle,
you haven't won the pools"

But meat to "Eggie" meant more pies,
more pies, in turn, more money
More cash, more bets, another step
closer to the honey

With the mindset of a drug dealer,
he mirrored their techniques
He could cut his meat, just like crack,
and make it last for weeks

But schemes and desperate rarely mix:
as poor old "Eggie" found
When he claimed his meat tray,
the meat was running round

A suckling pig, plump and moist:
as pig's go, 'twas a corker
But it wasn't coming quietly
and who could blame the porker

What found itself in "Eggie's" wares was,
if meat, long dead
He'd have to improvise, he thought,
and knock it on the head

He lured it with a stale baguette
and locked the bakery door
Chased it with a rolling pin,
but couldn't catch the boar

At last he had it cornered:
grabbed porkie in a pincer

But it thrashed and kicked, "Eggie" slipped
and both fell in the mincer

"Eggie's" wife arrived at dawn,
her turn to make the pies
Instead of dregs, A-grade mince;
imagine her surprise

She thought, "'Eggie's' had a win
and left this savoury filling"
Little did she realise,
the truth was far more chilling

She wrapped it in fresh pastry,
gave each a little scroll
"Eggie's" faith rewarded:
he was finally "on a roll"

He would have been delighted;
not a scrap of meat was wasted
Customers, unanimous,
the best they'd ever tasted

For once a pie to match its name,
and no liberties were taken
No-one could deny
it was truly "Egg and Bacon"

SANTA'S WORKING WEEKENDS IN THE WINDOW AT MYER

In the old days Santa
could make a decent living
The money didn't matter;
it was all about the giving

He was registered a charity,
but his book keeping was lax
The ATO determined
he owed a trillion dollars tax

Competition came from Amazon;
then the GFC
A hedge fund took him over,
he became an employee

Manufacturing and transport,
he knew every facet
But an audit classified him
as a non-performing asset

Santa was retrenched,
then re-hired as a contractor
When Mrs Claus complained
they cut her hours then sacked her

Santa contacted his union;
they made a lot of noise
But didn't want to jeopardise
the sweet deals for the boys

Can't let the needs of one

upset their cosy little club
So they called a stop work meeting
and adjourned it to the pub

Santa's salary was slashed
to reflect global supply
Based on average wages
at a sweat shop in Mumbai

Lost his holiday and sick leave,
other benefits as well
Had to pay for his own uniform
and they took away his bell

Removed his shift allowance,
claimed they didn't have the dough
Then paid a twenty million bonus
to the company's CEO

Sold the reindeer off for pet food,
which stirred a few emotions
Had Rudolph stuffed and mounted
for advertising and promotions

The elves were all laid off
and escorted from the site
Every grey beard hipster
sued for breach of copyright

They started making toys
from a blend of toxic waste
Branded it "organic"
to explain the bitter taste

When a newspaper exposed them

they sued for defamation
Changed "organic" to "all natural";
that's termed self-regulation

Put the squeeze on suppliers,
cut margins close to nil
While the CEO skimmed off
another fifteen mil

Moved Christmas back two months
to separate it from New Year
Transferred manufacture
in a deal with North Korea

Letters to Santa are
now sorted by machines
Then sold to a call centre
in The Philippines

It's their job to establish who's been naughty,
who's been nice
A judgement, not behaviour based,
but net return and price

A review by company lawyers
specifically forbade
Scaling rooves and chimneys,
Santa's usual stock in trade

There was Public Liability,
trespass and redress
It voided their insurance
and breached O H and S

His income, Santa pleaded,

wouldn't keep an elf alive
His boss threatened to replace him
with a Visa 245

Reclaim Australia was
having none of that
Reckon Santa must be Muslim,
with that beard and funny hat

They demanded the Air Force
turn Santa Claus away
"We might have stopped the boats,
now they're coming in by sleigh"

Santa always said he
would know when it was time
He'd outlived his usefulness
now Christmas was online

There were offers to relocate
to either Russia or Angola
But he couldn't take his costume
it was trademarked Coca-Cola

All the milk and chocolate biscuits
we left on the mantelpiece
Despite our good intentions
made him morbidly obese

All the beer and nips of whisky
had given him cirrhosis
Along with diabetes
and arteriolosclerosis

Thanks to Global Warming

his workshop's now a lake
Without the elves and reindeer,
where's the give, in give and take?

He subbied for the Tooth Fairy
but soon ran out of legs
The Easter Bunny let him go;
he kept eating all the eggs

For a while he tried busking
but couldn't give his all
Posing for the tourists
taking selfies in the mall

He sat down in the gutter,
thinking this is where it ends
All alone! Apart from
ninety million Facebook friends

Then he noticed a queue,
and laughter, long and loud
The Myer Christmas Windows
had drawn a massive crowd

The joy on children's faces;
a joy he'd thought long gone
In that moment, Santa realised,
the spirit still lives on

The sight of happy families
warmed him to his bones
They gazed into the window then shopped
next door at David Jones

Santa snuck around the back

and climbed into the display
Protected from the outside world;
you'll still find him there today

Another thousand years or so
he'll have the money to retire
That's why Santa's working weekends
in the window at Myer

SISTERS

Near thirty years, the Fraser sisters,
lived at number four
Having moved from interstate
not long after the war

Their modest clinker terrace
not much larger than a flat
A well kept cottage garden
and the obligatory cat

Manners, always faultless,
without having much to say
A brief exchange of pleasantries
then politely on their way

Not that Cyril Stokes, at number eight,
gave in without a try
All he'd get was
"Morning Cyril, lovely day, goodbye"

"No wonder they're both spinsters.
Who'd have them for wives?"
Eunice, his wife, would roll her eyes
and secretly envy their lives

A confidence shared with Cyril
at noon would circle the world by tea
Yet all he'd gleaned on the sisters
would fit on the wing of a flea

The more outgoing of the two,
the elder sister Viv

Ran a thriving tea room,
a few doors from "The Tiv"

Anne worked in millinery,
just down the road at Myer
Till a stroke in nineteen fifty eight
forced her to retire

Anne never quite recovered,
health in slow decline
Viv gave up the tea rooms
to care for her full time

She'd wheel Anne round the garden
when the roses were in bloom
Brush her hair and read to her,
when too ill to leave her room

"A nursing home" the doctor begged
"You'll die without respite"
Viv wouldn't hear a word of it,
nursed Annie, day and night

For a decade Viv looked after Anne
in their tiny maisonette
Not a skerrick of resentment;
not a moment of regret

Annie died in autumn,
barely sixty years of age
Viv spread her ashes
in a bed of Golden Sage

The remainder of her life,
Viv chose to live alone

Content to tend the garden,
rarely ventured far from home

The pastor at her funeral
spoke of selfless dedication
The worth of family values
and of moral inspiration

Her lawyer spoke less glowingly,
left carrying the can
Viv's will, drawn in the sixties,
bequeathed everything to Anne

Public records drew a blank,
no trace of next of kin
Till he found a hoard of papers
stored in a biscuit tin

The pair had different surnames:
different fathers, different mothers
There were no Fraser sisters –
Viv and Anne were lovers

In an era when their union
could have landed them in jail
They were forced to live a lie –
exist behind a veil

In these more enlightened times
would they be freed at last?
Or reconciled with platitudes –
assigned a lower caste

Without the right to marriage,
our reticence confirms

We acknowledge you as equals
but not on equal terms

We are yet to fully recognise,
that when push comes to shove
It's not about the gender –
it's all about the love

STARS

In the Mill's house, superstition
Dictated their routine
"Pig" stayed twelve for two years
To avoid turning thirteen

Without her daily stars
His Aunt Valma couldn't cope
Hard pushed to choose her undies
Without her precious horoscope

If her stars were looking dodgy
Valma's mood turned bleak
She'd climb under the blankets
And stay in bed all week

Wouldn't change a light bulb
Unless astrologers approved
When the bathroom mirror cracked
Valma sold the house and moved

"The stars are never wrong" she swore
Just look at great Aunt Bea
Ignored the stars and paid the price!
Dropped dead – at ninety three!"

"In my quest for love" she sighed
"They haven't failed me yet
Been married seven times, I have
How lucky can you get?"

An eighth marriage was annulled
Though stars cannot be blamed

Turned out to be a Scorpion
Not the Leo he had claimed

Then disaster fell upon her
Far worse than any spouse
Val dropped her umbrella
And it opened! – In the house!

When a black cat crossed her path
Val weakened at the knees
"I'm doomed" she wailed, "Beyond all hope
Bad luck comes in threes"

When Val ran out of milk
Things started to unravel
The shop was just across the street
But her stars said not to travel

Val tightly gripped a rabbit's foot
While trying to relax
Careful, as she crept
Not to step on any cracks

As Val came around the corner
She cried out it dismay
Across the path, a ladder
Completely blocked her way

Now to walk under a ladder
Is guaranteed bad luck
So Val stepped down the gutter
And was cleaned up by a truck

Still her horoscope was upbeat
Had she managed to survive

The truck, her favourite colour, red
And her lucky number five

"Avoid sudden confrontations
As Uranus squares with Mars"
But Val no longer needs her charts
She lives amongst the stars

TAKING REFUGE FROM THE ELEMENTS

The forecast, "Fine"; "Cold, but dry":
no mention of a gale
I'd dressed to keep the chill out,
not Arctic winds and hail

If nothing else the squall dispersed
the pall of acrid smog
I sheltered at a bus stop,
with an old man and his dog

I smiled a, "How's it going?"
both perfunctory and absurd
More acknowledgement than question,
though he took it at its word

He spoke for near an hour,
barely taking time to breathe
As though worried, a pause,
offered chance for me to leave

But I was going nowhere,
not that weather gave me choice
As he detailed his life
in the gentlest of voice

His bitser lay there sullenly,
head resting on one paw
Giving the impression she'd heard this
many times before

A story, laced with tragedy,
misfortune, hurt and loss

Though, if pity was his purpose,
it didn't come across

More a search for reason
in the telling of his tale
He'd found the perfect setting
in the lashings of the gale

Shunning hollow empathy,
I sat silent till the end
A stranger, to the lonely,
no more beloved friend

The tempest soon abated,
gone as quickly as it came
I watched the old man shuffle off –
the old man with no name

Sorrow shared finds comfort –
alone it brings despair
A storm unleashes havoc
but at least it clears the air

THE ELEMENTS

Four travellers met upon a field
Each claimed the path and would not yield

Earth, Air, Water, Fire
None would waiver, none retire

They argued long into the night
As to who deserved the right

Who was the greatest: who should lead?
Each thought themselves, at length agreed

To meet in council, face to face
Each, in turn, would forward their case

Despite their arrogance and pride
They'd let a simple vote decide

Earth, spoke first, dismissive, vain
Every comment dripped disdain

"Water: Your torrents merely tease
I tower above your lakes and seas"

"Your moody outbursts hold no fear
When seasons change, you disappear"

"Fire, you fool: your careless ways
All that gives you life, you raze"

"At least you're vibrant, unlike Air
Unless it moves, who'd know it's there?"

"I am solid, let others dream
It is I who reigns supreme"

Water, rose, could take no more
"Earth, you tiresome, pompous bore"

"I shaped you with my streams and creeks
My glaciers cleave your tallest peaks"

"As for Air, that fickle knave
It bears my clouds, like a galley slave"

"That peacock Fire, blustering flame
It flickers in panic at the sound of my name"

"Should I choose to descend, it could die
Who is the greatest? Clearly, 'tis I"

"Your Highness", sneered Fire
"let me bathe in your dew
I climb mountains — tell me, can you?"

"If I fear you so much, when we meet, tell me why
One kiss and you vanish, scurry back to the sky"

"Air, disorganized, changeable, irritating
I'm always ready but you keep me waiting"

"Earth, so lazy, you have no grounds to preach
Only move when you're pushed, like a whale on a
beach"

"You are nothing but dust when it's all said and done
The greatest among us? It's clear, I'm the one"

Air began gently, measured and slow
Breath quickly building and continued to blow

"Fire, so impatient, leaving too much to chance
I draw your flames, I make you dance"

"Earth, you act tough, yet are crumbs in my hands
I take fertile plains and create dessert sands"

"Dear Water, deluded, call me one of your slaves?
I fashion your currents, I shape your waves"

"You are powerless to stop me, I decide where you fall
It is beyond question – I'm the greatest of all"

And so they continued, without stopping to rest
Each considered themselves to be best

None would concede, none would back down
They wrestled and postured as they vied for the crown

The battle goes on, even now, as I'm writing
All round the world, ceaselessly fighting

A bushfire, an earthquake, a sandstorm, a gale
A cyclone, a mud slide, eruptions and hail

The world's made to suffer, for their selfish ambitions
They're in the wrong business – they'd make good
politicians

Elementary really·

TOWNS

"Delightful soup" quipped Joyce,
with a dry, sarcastic air
Beryl blushed with pride,
any praise from Joyce was rare

The praise was faint, at best,
had Beryl stopped to think it through
For she hadn't cooked a soup,
it was meant to be a stew

The town of Barry's Flat
was harmonious if slow
All that changed each March,
come the agricultural show

Friends, neighbours, families,
eyed each other with suspicion
Loyalties put on hold
due to fear of competition

There was a prize for best alpaca,
sheep, cattle, horses
Needlecraft, pot plants,
jams, preserves and sauces

Handmade soap, floral art,
scones and climbing beans
Waterfowl and lamingtons,
decoupage and nectarines

Rivalry was fierce,
allegiances upset

All for a ribbon
and a fifty cent rosette

Sabotage, bribery,
threats and accusations
Bullying, cheating
and outrageous allegations

Like weightlifters and cyclists
at the sharp end of their sport
The ones who hadn't cheated,
merely those they hadn't caught

Kingsley Backway's parsnips
looked an absolute delight
Till they realised they were carrot's
painted high gloss white

Archie Poon's giant Bantam hen,
had the trophy almost home
Till they found "she" was a rooster
with an amputated comb

Vi Quirk's swiss roll was stolen,
but no-one would confess
Unaware, deep inside,
Vi baked a GPS

She traced it to a mud cake,
entered by Vic Stone
He'd iced Vi's roll in chocolate
and claimed it as his own

In apples, Sandro Gauci
had his reputation tarnished

He claimed the rules said "non waxed" –
they didn't mention varnished

The Sheep Dog Trials fell foul
of one of Walter Thirkle's scams
He received all wethers,
while the rest were given rams

Jean Fidge's kelpie "Fudge"
was withdrawn when it went crackers
Jean discovered "Deep Heat"
had been rubbed into its knackers

The prize for biggest pumpkin
was a most coveted award
Sid Banks was reigning champion,
though some suspected fraud

Doc Cooch performed an autopsy,
which brought things to a head
While it proved to be a Queensland Blue,
its guts were filled with lead

A cow named "Dolly Parton"
had the spectators entranced
Sid Hobbs confessed its udders
had been surgically enhanced

Poor thing could hardly move
though its skin was smooth as silk
Botox in its teats
did nothing for the milk

They pulled the gum boot throwing,
amid grumblings of dissent

Stewards found Col Silbley's boot
half filled with cement

After Cec Higgs won the "Sheaf Toss",
they interviewed his wife
She proudly told them Cec had been
a tosser all his life

Tensions rose when Glenys Mears won
"Hand stitched cushion cover"
"I wouldn't wipe my arse with it"
and that came from her mother

Prue Tonks and Mavis Cuttle so incensed
they caused a blue
The judges fled the angry mob
locked in a port-a-loo

As for Joyce and her ambitions,
they ended in disgrace
Carelessness left egg, well,
mostly whipped cream on her face

Seems her Coconut Crème Pie,
wasn't all it claimed to be
Joyce overlooked the label,
"Baked by Sara Lee"

While Beryl and her "Vegie Stew"
supplied the day's surprise
The judges were unanimous,
awarding it first prize

Her dignity held firm,
while those around her chose to stoop

Thanks to Joyce's snide remark,
Beryl's stew was crowned "Best soup"

And so the show was over,
at least for another year
Trophies languished under beds,
no longer held so dear

Life returned to normal,
and tensions settled down
There's Barry's Flat in all of us,
for the world is one big town

TWO VERBS

King Street.
I was sitting in the squad car watching the flotsam
and jetsam spill out of the clubs.
The call came in at 2am.
Another sentence butchered, the third in a week.
Same M.O. as the others – strangled by a dangling
participle.

The first victim was discovered in an Armadale
Antique shop.
It read "Mahogany Chippendale Drawers; would suit
lady with thick legs and brass knockers."
No one cares about grammar any more.
Most wouldn't know a heteronym form a homophone.

Later that day we captured a mutilated modifier on
the wall of a Hume Highway truck stop.
I'll never forget that sign
"Chicken Parmiagana $12, Fish and Chips $15,
Children $6"
There are some sickos out there.

We had an unconfirmed report of a Full Stop missing
from a playground car park.
"Slow Children Crossing". We searched but found no
sign – no fast children either.
I was just about to head to The Lomond for a nightcap
when I picked up a Code 26 on the radio.

A group of mixed metaphors had been ambushed by a
gang of oxymorons on Chapel Street – I knew their
type – strictly lower case, a comma short of a semi
colon.
Uniform said there were bodies everywhere.

I raced straight to the scene hoping to arrive before
the remains could be disturbed but I was too late.
The consonants had all scattered and someone had
emptied their vowels.
It was not a pretty sight.

I rounded up all the words and separated them into
nouns, verbs, adverbs, pronouns and minority groups
such as indefinite articles, quantifiers and
pre-determiners, and interrogated them one syllable
at a time.

Like the rest of the world the force has gone PC –
you're not supposed to profile based on word type
anymore, but I'm old school, I call an acronym an
acronym – or A.C.R.O.N.Y.M. for short.

Take nouns for example – they're all the same, only
want to talk about themselves; shallow and
predictable.

Pronouns, adverbs – they talk big but they're nothing
on their own.

Adjectives – all fluff. A lot of pretty words that spend
too much time brown nosing nouns – creepy little
crawlers.

But verbs, they're always where the action is. Where
there's trouble, you'll find a verb close by.
I don't trust them – never have.
They lie and they cheat.
They might say "barter'" but they mean "steal"
"Discuss" but they mean "murder"

After forty years of dealing with lower case scum I can
smell a dishonest verb ten paragraphs away and there
were two verbs in this lot that smelt worse than an
obsolete subjunctive.

Falsify and Swindle.
They tried to pass themselves off as nouns but I was
on to them – and they knew if they were caught I'd
throw the dictionary at them.

The mood was tense – past, present and future.
Swindle tried to buy me off by grassing a couple of
filthy limericks.
I said, "Is that a preposition?"
"No" he growled, "that" is a pronoun"

I advised him not to get smart
"But I already got Get Smart on DVD" he replied
"You already "have" Get Smart" I corrected
"I just told you I got it Copper " he snapped
I was getting nowhere

While I was taking a statement from a sad old cliché,
Falsify and Swindle made a break for the Thesaurus.
If they made it inside I'd never see them again.
I hemmed them in with parentheses, but they escaped
over the top, taking a comma with them.

The time for punctuation was over.
I realised there'd be collateral damage, but I had no choice.

I sprayed them all with correction fluid.
A lot of good words were deleted that day
honest, hardworking words that had never willingly
been anywhere near a Murdoch publication.

There was an investigation, of course.
The sole surviving apostrophe claimed it had been
verballed, but there was a big question mark hanging
over its credibility. Lucky I hadn't deleted that as
well.

I was cleared but the writing was on the wall – damn
graffiti.
I'd always lived by the alphabet – I was happy to
watch my "P's and Q's" but I was too old for "LOL and
53X".

I took early retirement and now play Sunday's 4 to 6
at Barney Allen's in Fitzroy St Kilda with Dave Moll,
another ex-detective from the Bad Grammar Squad.

So next time you see a "disabled toilet" ask yourself,
"Why doesn't somebody fix it?"
And remember - Never trust a verb – they're always
up to something.

VEGAN BBQ

"That? On the barbie? Ha!
Not a snowball's hope in hell!"
Uncle Kevin's verdict
Rang as clear as any bell

"Nothing against you veggies
Let me get that straight
But no way those chickpea what's its
Are going near my grate"

Kevin's nephew, Tristan
Was a lad endowed with passion
But Kevin knew his principles
Had more to do with fashion

Last month "Psychic Healing"
"Re-birthing" weeks before
Now he's "Ovo-bloody-lacto"
Some breed of herbivore

Ditched KFC for TVP
Rump for Tofu Steak
Scrubbed Kanye from his mp3
Replaced him with Nick Drake

He'd brought along a friend
Doing Arts at Melbourne Uni
"Bloody Arts" sneered Kev
"Another left wing loony"

On their T-shirts "Meat is murder"
On the back "Thou shalt not kill"

Kev scoffed "They want the compost heap
Not the bloody grill"

"Combing through the salads
Plucking leaves, seeds and shoots
Sporting leather jackets
And red Doc Martin boots"

Kevin bit his tongue
His patience wearing thin
"Won't eat the flesh" he snarled
"But they'll wear the bloody skin"

Kevin's wife Kayleen barked
"You cynical old prick
Cook the boys some tofu Kev
And make it bloody quick"

"But petal" whimpered Kevin
"It'll stuff the cast iron plate"
"You'll be stuffed" Kayleen snapped
"If you don't get cracking mate"

"No "snuggles" in the morning
If those lads don't get a feed"
Kev knew what "no snuggles" meant
And reluctantly agreed

Now, the barbie can get ugly
As all carnivores would know
A sea of molten fat and grease
Nowhere for it to go

Seeping from the chop tails
Oozing from the snags

Corroding deck and burners
Reducing clothes to rags

Kev snatched a mung bean burger
And flung it on the top
It landed with a splash
Between a rissole and a chop

Something magic happened
As it sank into the grunge
It sucked up twice its weight in fat
Just like a kitchen sponge

Kev chucked on several more and gasped
"Will wonders never cease?
They've hoovered clean the hotplate
Soaked up all the grease"

Kevin was astounded
But chose to keep it quiet
He might miss out on his "snuggles"
And cause a vegan riot

"Best veggie burgers ever"
So his nephew Tristan reckons
His friend it seems concurred
They both came back for seconds

Kayleen seemed impressed
Kev thought "Hello, I'm in luck"
As Kayleen cooed "come on pet
How 'bout a quick Cold Duck?"

Kevin popped the cork
Even scored a little kiss

He was going to share his secret but well,
"Ignorance is bliss"

Tristan bailed his uncle
With an air that oozed conceit
"I told you Uncle Kev" he crowed
"They taste as good as meat"

"I'll give you that" thought Kevin
"And a hundred times more fatty
Each contains more cow
Than a half pound minced beef patty"

Still, Kevin was converted
And remains so to this day
At his barbies, the mung beans
Are the first thing in the tray

He loves his veggie burgers
Reckons you can't beat'em
"The best thing on the grill" he swears
"Providing you don't eat'em"

WASHING

A great idea, in theory;
we both come out a winner
One night you do the washing up,
next you cook the dinner

You expect teething problems;
fine tune and reassess
There are some minor issues
I'm eager to address

Now I know it says they're ready cooked,
I've taken that on board
But fish fingers and frozen chips
taste better when they're thawed

No doubt your mum can cook
and does omelettes very well
But when she said four eggs
I don't think she meant the shell

Don't think that I'm complaining;
I like baked beans on toast
But why use a baking dish?
It's not a bloody roast

Please don't use the microwave
to dry your jocks and socks
Yes, frozen pizza's fine –
but first remove it from the box

While scourers are effective
it should probably be noted

Not the wisest option
when the pan is Teflon coated

While I'm on that subject,
not a personal attack
Teflon coated pans —
you don't scrape off the black!

I've mentioned this before
but I'll give you a reminder
You can't clean the oven — ever!
With an angle grinder

While a drill for a whisk
is resourceful I admit
It would have caused less damage
if you'd taken out the bit

I applaud all acts of cleanliness;
not trying to give you grief
But the coffee plunger's not the place
for soaking your false teeth

I empathise, washing up,
everybody loathes
But the washing machine's designed
exclusively for clothes

You may have wrapped the plates in a towel
before you put them in
You might have even got away with soak
but pushed your luck with spin

I hope you're not offended
by my personal critiquing

Our arrangement will improve
with a little bit of tweaking

So tonight I'll cook, your turn to wash,
let's have no more debates
I'll get Chinese take away,
you get paper plates

AFTERWARD

THE HEART OF ST KILDA

The heart of St Kilda

The market? The Mission? The gardens? The pier?
The Bowlo? The Espy? Veg Out? – or here?

A blending of cultures, texture and tone
Flavours infused; but its style is its own

Coffee, a beer, rum balls and strudels
Lemongrass, pasta, tapas and noodles

Brioche, calamari, kebabs, GHB
A screaming orgasm or a chamomile tea

Posses of cyclists; cars by the jam
The Scenic Railway – the 96 tram

St Kilda's a city – not in part, but complete
Where the homeless and wealthy walk the same street

The heart of St Kilda

Breakfast at midnight – A night cap at noon
A Mirka Mora mural – A Fred Negro cartoon

A nightclub, a concert, the ballet, a rave
Adapting to fashion - but never its slave

Ugly, at times – conflicts and frictions
A city of contrast and at times contradictions

Board shorts, thongs – or resplendent in drag

A penthouse apartment or a brown paper bag
A hoody, denim or gold lamé
Assuredly straight – yet, comfortably gay

Contemporary, classical, modest and bold
Here they welcome the new – but will fight for the old

Live and let live – but won't shirk confrontation
When culture locks horns with gentrification

As much cabaret as it is rock'n'roll
You may fluff with its makeup – but never it's soul

The heart of St Kilda

The music – nurtured, inspired and avowed
Dianna, Kiss, Roland S Howard,
Rosie, Ruby, Kelly and more
I Spit On Your Gravy, The Boys Next Door

Writers, Accountants, Students, Musicians
Nurses, Artists, Beauty Technicians
Backpackers, Buskers, Shopkeepers, Goths
Bogans, Vegans, Pensioners, Toffs

Baristas, Barristers, Soliciters, Solicitors
Parallel worlds behind the lights and applause

The homeless, the damaged, dispossessed, self
inflicted
Those who've lost hope, the abused, the addicted

Are met, not in judgement, not in shame or despair
The true heart of St Kilda – is the people who care

SULPHER CREEK

Grand Final day at Sulphur Creek
The mood at best, was tense
The medics carried mace
Barbed wire secured the fence

The Razor Hill Vultures
Were are a vicious bunch of thugs
The Captain, Coach and President
On bail for dealing drugs

The Coffin Bay Boners
Would kill before defeat
All worked at the abattoir
And were used to carving meat

"Suckhole" Spragg, "Agro" Cline
And Tarquin "Choirboy" Kronk
"Bonehead" Greeves, "Snowball" Filch
And one simply known as "Gronk"

Stan Gooch had only umpired
Seven games in the reserves
But they needed someone tough
Who wasn't prone to nerves

Stan was just the ticket
With the build for contact sports
Picture Kim Beasley's arse
In Warwick Capper's shorts

Before the ball was bounced
There was mayhem all around

Two Vultures and a Boner
Lay unconscious on the ground

When Stanley blew his whistle
All the players did was scoff
He appealed to both the captains
They told him to piss off

He had to take control
Or he'd never get it back
So he charged in like a rugby prop
And split apart the pack

"I'll say this once," barked Stan
"So listen up you turds
I'm giving you the facts
So better mark my words"

"To you I'm just an ump
But Proctology's my profession
I'm an expert in arseholes
If you'll pardon the expression"

"I've seen skinny, fat and hairy
Loose, tight and torn
But the arsehole I can't handle
Is still waiting to be born"

"So you arseholes go in hard
The way it should be played
But cross the line you'll find out
How well I know my trade"

The opening was a cracker
Both sides played the ball

A bit of argie-bargie
Jumper holding, that was all

Quarter time, all tied up
Best game in years, they reckoned
The Boner's "Ferret" Burns
Slotted three to start the second

"Filthy" Frank Fasalo
Decked Burns behind the play
A fifty metre penalty
And the Boner's kicked away

A "Hitman" Harme's torpedo
Put the Boners up by five
But "Weasel" Belcher's snap
Kept the Vultures hopes alive

Third term, honours even
Neither side could get the jump
Tempers sort of held in check
All credit to the ump

Stan didn't muck around
When Gaylord Munce was floored
The fifty metre count
Stretched from full back to full forward

The final quarter started
With a goal from "Veggie" French
The Boners coach went berko
Dragging "Bonehead" to the bench

When "Hatchet" Hobbs was nabbed
For pulling "Mullet" Fisher's hair

"Mullet" kicked a pearler
And the match was back to square

The game was on a knife edge
A premiership at stake
No-one gave a stuff
How many rules they had to break

Lester "Bluetongue" Izzard
Was as mad as he was crude
So proud of his nickname
He had his tongue tattooed

Couldn't kick or handball
Didn't even train
His talents lay inflicting
Excruciating pain

He'd barely left the bench
Nothing done by halves
He ran his boot stops down the back
Of "Snowball" Filch's calves

"Daggers" Sharp did his bit
To even up the odds
As "Ferret" pulled his socks up
"Daggers" kneed him in the cods

While "Suckhole" Spragg punched
The bejesus out of "Vegie"
"Hatchet" snuck behind
And performed the perfect wedgie

As "Veg" tried to extricate
His shorts from up his crack

"Bluetongue" seized the moment
And sunk his teeth into his sack

The fighting escalated
Spread from goal to goal
The umpires tried their best
But could not regain control

Eye gouging, head butting
Kicking, biting, tripping
Elbows, coat hangers
King hits and squirrel gripping

Stan growled, "I warned these arseholes
Now I'm fed up to the gills
It's time I introduced them
To my non-umpiring skills"

He leapt into the melee
No interest in debate
Licked his index finger
And shoved it right up "Bluetongue's" date

"Bluetongue" froze rigid
Like a "Peters Cream Between"
Stan had entered territory
No man had ever been

"Veg" saw his chance
To retrieve his half chewed knacker
Stan was back in charge
Took the game by the clacker

He gave a twist or two
"Bluetongue's" eyes glazed like glass

Just a day at work for Stan
Finger up an arse

"These big macho bruisers"
He used to tell his mum
"Curl up like little puppies
When a finger's up their bum"

Stan had a theory
Why most blokes try to pike it
They were scared, so he reckoned
Scared they might just like it

The players stood there stunned
A bewildered, eerie, silence
No-one quite knew what to do
They were used to "healthy" violence

"Hands up anybody else
Who wants their prostate checked?"
"Muck around again" cried Stan
"You know what to expect"

The remainder of the game
Was played well within the law
The sides traded goals
And the match wound up a draw

The coach's went bananas
"That was way outside the rules"
Stan cried "So are shirt fronts,
I'm not tolerating fools"

Now there's scope within the rule book
For some interpretation

But nowhere does in mention
Rectal examination

"You're all washed up" they told him
But that didn't worry Stan
"Too much like work" he huffed
As he copped a lifetime ban

Clearly his behaviour
Was improper, irrespective
But no-one could deny
It was spectacularly effective

Think outside the square
You can accomplish anything
Stan thought outside the square alright
He thought inside the ring

There's a message in this sordid tale
The message is "neglect
Your arsehole, like your nails and hair
Deserves the same respect"

You blokes who don't like doctors
I know just how you feel
But if it helps to keep you healthy
Well, the finger's no big deal

There's one thing in this life
As sure as tax and death
You'll cop it up the freckle
If you stick it up the ref

58603439R00099

Made in the USA
Charleston, SC
16 July 2016